CHOOSING A CHURCH

A BIBLICAL AND PRACTICAL GUIDE

JONATHAN STODDARD

CONTENTS

I've known Jon Stoddard for years. We've worked closely together and prayed together many times. It is evident in his prayers and practice that he loves the Church. Not simply his church or denomination, but Christ's Church locally and worldwide. *Choosing a Church* is evidence of this love in print. Jon has provided us with a guide that is biblical, practical, Gospel-centered, and reaches across denominational lines. As a pastor in Utah where so many people I meet and minister to are floundering in their search for a biblical church they can call home, this is a wonderful resource to hand them. Jon has done the entire Christian Church a great service in providing this guide. —Tim Barton, Pastor, Grace Church of Utah

This book helped me tremendously as I was transitioning out of the Mormon faith. Like Jon mentions in the introduction, I too am a person of lists and spreadsheets. If not for this book forcing me to take a step back and reevaluate

the essentials, I would probably still be wandering from church to church looking for the perfect one.
—Daniel Harper, Network Services Specialist, West Jordan, Utah

Choosing a Church is a great introduction for those who are interested in Christianity but don't know where to turn. Jon Stoddard has frequent conversations with people looking for a new spiritual home. He has boiled down the wisdom he has gained into this concise handbook, where he skillfully applies theological and historical depth to answer the questions those without a background in the Christian faith are most likely to have.
—Ross Anderson, Teaching Pastor, Alpine Church, Author, *Understanding Your Mormon Neighbor*

In my work on the university campus, I am desperate for resources to help non-Christian, un-churched, or de-churched students navigate the world of church for the first time. *Choosing a Church* is concise, insightful, and thoughtfully practical. I would be happy to give this book to any of my students.
—Brian Tsui, Reformed University Fellowship campus minister, San Jose State University

I wish I'd found this book right after I left the LDS Church. Jon offers a helpful explanation for why there are so many different churches, and why that's actually a good thing. Winsomely, he doesn't just recommend his own church or denomination, but helps you navigate the

pitfalls to find the kind of faithful biblical church that may be right for you.
—Joey Day, Software Engineer, Draper, Utah

Many people today struggle with even knowing what they should be looking for in a church, let alone going through that process when going through a transition. *Choosing a Church* is a practical guide written by Pastor Jon Stoddard who has personally seen many people wrestle with this very issue in Utah and elsewhere. This is a book for someone who wants to actually think biblically about the process and not just find the church with the best coffee. Highly recommended!
—Doug McNutt, Pastor, Gospel Church, Utah

Choosing a Church should appeal to anyone looking for a concise read that boils down the essentials of church-finding. In this little book, Stoddard provides a fresh and much-needed perspective, steering clear of denominational and theological thickets. It's not only for those who are searching for a church, but for those who wish to evaluate their local church's present ministry. Laypeople and leaders would benefit greatly from reviewing these unifying principles that all Christ-centered churches ought to hold in common.
—Bryan Lee, Owner of Sparrow Electric, Pastor of Worship, Jordan Valley Church, Utah

Finding the right church is always a challenge. Stoddard offers a great framework to help you find a church. He is able to articulate the nuances and differences of worship styles and denominations while staying faithful to the call of unity of the Church as a whole. Stoddard does justice to the diversity of the Church while remaining true to finding a church that embodies the Gospel, regardless of its denomination or style. If you're looking for a guide that will help you find a church right for you, this is a great resource.

—Paul Stoddard, Operations Analyst, Goldman Sachs

Finding a church to call home is never an easy decision, but it is an important one. Jonathan Stoddard provides thoughtful, biblical guidance and answers to important questions for those wondering how they should choose a church.

—Jeffrey Kerr, Pastor, Crestwood Presbyterian Church, Edmonton, Alberta

Published by White Blackbird Books, an imprint of Storied Publishing.

Permission requests and other questions may be directed to the Contact page at www.storied.pub.

Scriptures taken from the Holy Bible, New International Version®, NIV®. Copyright © 1973, 1978, 1984, 2011 by Biblica, Inc.™ Used by permission of Zondervan. All rights reserved worldwide. www.zondervan.com The "NIV" and "New International Version" are trademarks registered in the United States Patent and Trademark Office by Biblica, Inc.™

ISBN-13: 978-0-9973984-8-9

This book was previously printed under the same title by JVC Press. Parts have been updated and edited. Printed by White Blackbird Books with permission.

Cover design by Sean Benesh

The White Blackbird image is adapted from a painting by Erin Shaw and is used by permission. Shawart.com.

ABOUT WHITE BLACKBIRD BOOKS

White blackbirds are extremely rare, but they are real. They are blackbirds that have turned white over the years as their feathers have come in and out over and over again. They are a redemptive picture of something you would never expect to see but that has slowly come into existence over time.

There is plenty of hurt and brokenness in the world. There is the hopelessness that comes in the midst of lost jobs, lost health, lost homes, lost marriages, lost children, lost parents, lost dreams, loss.

But there also are many white blackbirds. There are healed marriages, children who come home, friends who are reconciled. There are hurts healed, children fostered and adopted, communities restored. Some would call these events entirely natural, but really they are unexpected miracles.

The books in this series are not commentaries, nor are they crammed with unique insights. Rather, they are a collage of biblical truth applied to current times and places. The authors share their poverty and trust the Lord to use their words to strengthen and encourage his people.

May this series help you in your quest to know Christ as he is found in the Gospel through the Scriptures. May you look for and even expect the rare white blackbirds of God's redemption through Christ in your midst. May you be thankful when you look down and see your feathers have turned. May you also rejoice when you see that others have been unexpectedly transformed by Jesus.

PREFACE

This book came about because I was tired of being asked, "What do Presbyterians believe?" It bothered me that I didn't have a good answer. I could give a dull, rambling answer that probably made people wonder why I was Presbyterian. I could talk about the history of our denomination, how we were different from other Presbyterian churches, and how we were like many other evangelical churches. But people's eyes would glaze over before I got to the interesting parts.

I realized the question beneath the question was really, "How do I find a church for me?" Teaching them the differences between Old Light and New Light Presbyterians did little to help anyone figure out if my church would be a good one for them. Actually, such an answer probably confirmed that this was not the right church!

People really want to know if this is a church where they can fit in. Is this a church where they can grow? Will we hear about Jesus? Will we be loved and accepted?

I'm the pastor of a small church in Utah. (Perhaps you're not surprised given that I couldn't even answer the question about what Presbyterians believe!) But even in our small church we get a steady stream of visitors, many who are undergoing a major faith transition. As I had more and more conversations with these people I realized they were often confused, frustrated, and wishing they had a way to navigate all the different types of churches out there.

And so I started writing this booklet. Many people's questions were similar. Many (though not all) were coming out of a Mormon/Latter Day Saints (LDS) church background. I've written this booklet with particular sensitivity to the issues and questions of those coming out of the LDS faith.

This book would not have been written without the help of so many people. First, I want to thank all those willing to ask their questions and share their struggles in finding a church. I've written this for people like you so that your journey to find a church will be as easy as possible.

I want to thank Tim Barton, Joey Day, Daniel Harper, Doug McNutt, Rich Sandford, and Paul Stoddard for taking the time to read this book and offer comments and feedback. I also want to thank Naomi Winebrenner. Without her skilled editing what is written here would be much less readable.

Finally, I want to thank my wife, Lisa, for her constant encouragement and belief that I have something to say that will be helpful to others. I'm deeply indebted to her.

In Christ,
    Jonathan Stoddard
    West Jordan, Utah

INTRODUCTION

Finding a church is difficult. I usually start out excited. I listen to sermons online. I make lists. I've even made spreadsheets. I love spreadsheets! But soon I find myself tired of looking. Weeks turn into months, and I want to settle down. My excitement gives way to frustration (how do I know if I've found *the one*?) and disappointment (no church seems to be a perfect fit). Soon I just want to find a place where I can become part of the community instead of just a passerby.

Church labels can be confusing. You can visit a Presbyterian church with robes and hymnals and another Presbyterian church with screens and hipsters. It can get overwhelming to sort through the differences between Methodists, Baptists, Pentecostals, and Anglicans. What gives? And what about all those buzzwords people use to describe churches: emergent, traditional, ancient-future, contemporary, and blended. Is this church seeker-sensitive? Sometimes you can feel like you are ordering a smoothie: "I'd like a traditional, double blended, organic smoothie. Oh, I mean um... worship service." And why do we need labels for a church? Can't I just go to a Christian church?

Did you know that someone has published a book listing every denomination? It's more than 400 pages long. Good luck using that to help you find a church! You'll die before you get to the end of the book.

For so many in Utah, this question, "How do I know what church to attend?" has historical significance. A young Joseph Smith was struggling with that same question. He asked the question many ask: "If there is only one God and one Bible, why so many different denominations?" This led Joseph to create a new church, which, presumably, he believed was the correct one.

Others have not received an answer to this question. Perhaps you should just go with what's oldest and join a Catholic church. But how do you know it is still faithful to Jesus' message?

If there is such a thing as a true Church, what does it look like? Some have argued the boundaries of the true Church line up with one particular denomination. Others see the true Church as defined by adherence to certain theological creeds. Others simply seek no other creed than the Bible, and that defines the true Church.

Like I said, finding a church is confusing!

My hope is as you work through this book you will gain confidence as you search for the right church for you. Because being part of a church is important. The Church is what Christ laid down his life for. The Church is God's instrument for bringing Christ to all of creation. The Church is like the portal between heaven and earth. The Church is the place where Christ is at work making all things new. The Church is where the action is.

I love the Church, and I hope you will too!

WHY CHOOSE A CHURCH?

The rest of this book rests on a single presupposition: you want to be part of a church. You've likely picked up this book because you have some interest in finding a church. But perhaps you're not sure. Many people question the value of the institutional church today. I regularly hear people say, "I believe in God and pray, but I don't feel the need to go to church." Why should you bother to commit to a church? Let me list a few reasons.

Without Commitment It's Hard to Grow

If you want to become really good at a sport you need a coach. You need someone on the outside to hold you accountable to your goals, to see things you cannot see, and to give corrective feedback. When you don't feel like getting up early to practice, knowing you have a coach waiting for you motivates you. When you are shifting your weight in a way that you can't notice, a coach can quickly notice the problem.

Our spiritual growth is similar. Paul tells us the way we grow in Christ is by *"speaking the truth in love"* to one another (Eph 4:15–16). For someone to speak the truth in love to you, he or she needs to know you. Part of committing to one church is to be known by others who can help you grow.

You Have Something to Offer

Ultimately, it is selfish to withhold your God-given spiritual gifts from fellow believers. Each person has something to offer for the blessing of others. While you can volunteer here or there outside of church, there is no other place where you can regularly use those gifts to bless others. The Church is a community, and a community is healthy when everyone is helping one another.

God Loves the Church

If we love Jesus, we will love what Jesus loves, and Jesus loves the Church. He loves the Church so much he died for her (Eph 4:25). Sometimes we are hurt by churches, or they disappoint us. The Church has also hurt Jesus, yet he lay down his life for her. For someone to say, "I'm a Christian, but not part of a church," is to ultimately say, "I'm a Christian, but I don't follow Christ." How so? Because Christ is the head of his Church. Christ is found in his Church.

In Revelation 7 we see a picture of heaven. A great multitude of people from all over the world join together in worship. When we gather with others for worship, we are actually gathering with all the angels before God's heavenly throne (Heb 12:18–24). This means when we are gathered together for worship we are the closest to heaven we will be on this earth.

No church is perfect. No church lives up to these ideals. There are an unfortunate number of people who have been deeply hurt by their churches. But we cannot let these things keep us from understanding God's design for the Church. When the Church is being faithful to God, it is an awesome place to be!

WHAT MAKES A TRUE CHURCH?

How do you know if a church is being faithful to God? Catholics, Presbyterians, Mormons, Baptists, Independents, and Jehovah's Witnesses all say they are true Churches. Yet these churches can also hold theological views that contradict each other.

Fortunately, the Bible gives us some principles for understanding what constitutes a true Church. In Matthew 16, Jesus asks Peter who he thinks he is. Peter responds by saying, *"You are the Messiah, the Son of the living God"* (Matt 16:16, New International Version)[1]. Pleased with this answer, Jesus responds by saying:

> *And I tell you that you are Peter, and on this rock I will build my church, and the gates of Hades will not overcome it. I will give you the keys of the kingdom of heaven; whatever you bind on earth will be bound in heaven, and whatever you loose on earth will be loosed in heaven.* (Matt 16:18–19)

This passage contains the foundation for the Church as we know it today. It starts with Peter when Jesus gives Peter the keys of the kingdom.

As the leader, Peter will have power to control who comes in and out of the Church. So we must say that any true Church must be able to trace its authority back to Peter.

And indeed churches do this in various ways. The Catholic Church claims this through apostolic succession, so that the current pope is the Vicar of St. Peter. The LDS Church does this through Joseph Smith, who claimed to receive this authority from Jesus after it had been lost after the Apostles. Most churches that came out of the Reformation do this by tying it to the apostolic teaching. How should a church trace its authority back to Peter?

One passage often left out of this discussion occurs just a few verses later. In Matthew 16:18 Jesus promises to build his Church upon Peter. Yet in Matthew 16:23 Jesus says to Peter, *"Get behind me, Satan!"* This passage presents some difficulties for those who would want to tie the apostolic authority to a particular person. Because here it appears Peter lost it!

Jesus said the gates of hell will not prevail against the Church, but now the rock the Church is built upon is called Satan. If the apostolic authority is tied to Peter personally, it calls into question the truth of Jesus' claim that nothing will stop the Church.

However, if we see that apostolic authority is tied to

apostolic doctrine and not to a particular person, we can make better sense of everything going on. Peter's confession of true doctrine preceded his apostolic authority. When he strayed from Jesus's teaching, he strayed from his apostolic authority. The other apostles made a profession that Jesus is the Messiah, and they also have this apostolic authority (Matt 18:18). All this fits with Paul's explanation that the Church is built upon the foundation of the apostles and prophets (Eph 2:20).

What is the primary role of the apostles? To be witnesses for Christ (Acts 1:8). Therefore we are part of Christ's Church when we stand upon the teaching that the apostles established as the witnesses of Christ and his ministry.

What Did the Apostles Teach?

If the true Church is found where the apostolic teachings are taught, what are the apostolic teachings? In one helpful passage, Paul speaks of unity in the Church and then lists seven things that he describes as "one." These, then, seem to describe the boundaries of Christian unity:

> *Make every effort to keep the unity of the Spirit through the bond of peace. There is one body and one Spirit, just as you were called to one hope when you were called; one Lord, one faith, one baptism; one God and Father of all, who is over all and through all and in all.* (Eph 4:3–6)

First notice that we do not create unity, but we maintain it. When we profess faith in Christ we are baptized into the one body of Christ (1 Cor 11). Thus unity is established. The unity is something that we can lose. How? Ephesians 4:4–6 gives us examples. The word "one" is used seven times. By straying from these key things, we lose our unity. Let's look at some of the key aspects of unity that Paul lists:

- *one body and spirit*

This refers to the one body of Christ that has been given the Spirit of Christ. This body is the Church. There is only one Church, and Christ is head of that Church. This Church may take different forms and meet in different locations, but it is part of the one Church. Perhaps we could think of it like a modern conglomerate corporation. Pizza Hut, Kentucky Fried Chicken, and Taco Bell are all owned by the same parent company. They have different logos, locations, and even employee rules, yet they all belong to the same corporate entity. They are one company that files one tax return. The Church is similar. We can take different forms, shapes, and sizes. Yet from God's perspective, we are all part of the same parent company.

- *one hope*

Christians are united in our hope–that God will one

day live with his people in harmony forever, and they will reflect the very glory of Christ.

- *one Lord*

In the New Testament the term *Lord* often refers to Jesus Christ. Unity in the Church is based upon Jesus Christ as the only way to the Father (John 14:6).

- *one faith*

The object of every Christian's faith is God himself. One who puts his or her faith in something else does not share the same unity of believers.

- *one baptism*

Baptism is the mark of entrance into the universal Church, not a particular church. A Baptist coming to a Presbyterian church does not need to be baptized again. Neither ought a Presbyterian going to a Lutheran church be re-baptized. Baptism is the mark of entrance into Christ's Church, in whatever form it takes. If a church requires you to be re-baptized, it may indicate that it differs in aspects of Christian unity.[2]

- *one God and Father*

The combination of these terms gives us an important

reminder of God's transcendence (his bigness) and immanence (his closeness). Often people are tempted to
emphasize one of these over the other. The person who
believes God exists but doesn't interfere with the dealings
of people has forgotten about his immanence. God gets
close to his people, most notably in the person and word
of Jesus Christ who was born into this world and walked
among us. The person who sees God as just like us, only
bigger and more powerful, has forgotten about his transcendence. God is wholly above us. He created all there
is and stands outside of time. He holds the universe in the
palm of his hand.

We need both transcendence and immanence. God is
our loving Father, and he is Holy, Holy, Holy. When we
do not hold both, we risk losing our Christian unity.

Who Determines Essential Doctrine?

Our study has shown that apostolic authority is tied to
apostolic teaching and doctrine. Wherever true doctrine
is being taught, there is a true Church.

Doctrine is a scary word for some. When we start
talking about doctrine, some plug their ears and say, "I
only believe Jesus." Such a response often comes as a
reaction from and incorrect understanding of doctrine.

Webster's dictionary simply defines doctrine as "a set
of ideas or beliefs that are taught or believed to be true."
When we understand this basic definition, we should see
that *everyone* holds a doctrine. I've yet to meet anyone

who believes nothing to be true. If someone believed nothing to be true, that would in essence be their doctrine. Even saying "I only believe in Jesus" is a simple theological doctrinal statement.

From our examination of Ephesians 4, we see Paul does not attribute equal importance to every little thing in Scripture. Paul highlights seven things that are key to unity. That Paul sees certain Christian doctrines as of first importance (1 Cor 15:3ff) implies that other doctrines are of lesser importance. But how do you know which doctrines are of first importance and which are of lesser importance?

Paul has given us a good foundation in Ephesians 4, where he lists seven key doctrines that we must be united on. The problem is that when we read Scripture, there is always a level of interpretation. So my interpretation of what Paul means when he says "one God" may mean something different to me than it means to you. Who is right?

Our first rule for interpretation is that we should let Scripture speak on its own terms. This means we should let Scripture interpret Scripture. If there is one divine author of Scripture, we can often get clarity in understanding what one particular part of Scripture says by looking at what it says about that same topic in other places.

But this still leaves room for various interpretation. So we could then frame the question this way: "Who controls what essential doctrine is?" This gets to the heart of the issue, and there are various answers to this question.

Let's examine the most common ways to answer this question of control.

The Individual Determines Essential Doctrine

Most people in the United States probably believe something like, "No church or creed or group of elites should tell me what doctrine is correct or not." When someone says he believes in no creed but the Bible, ultimately what he is saying is that his own interpretation of the Bible is what he believes. This appeals to our independent American culture.

But there are a couple of problems with this view. First, it's hard to maintain Christian unity when you do this. Your interpretation of the Bible is certainly going to differ from others. Without a summary of your beliefs, it's hard to really know what you believe. In fact, even those who adhere to no creed but the Bible still make use of creedal concepts. Many Christians would speak of the importance of believing in the Trinity[3], though the word "Trinity" is not found in Scripture. It's like a one-word creed that describes something we see in Scripture regarding the unity and diversity of God. It's incredibly hard to not make use of creedal-type language when speaking about beliefs.

Another serious issue with this belief is that, as much as we may want to think it, we are not nearly as independent as we wish. We grew up in a particular environment, and that background had a huge influence on us. And so when we go to interpret Scripture (as unbiased as we wish to think we are), our environment and background impact how we interpret Scripture.

I recently traveled to Kenya, and while eating dinner with a local family we started talking about our mothers-in-law. I said that my mother-in-law lives just down the street from us. It takes about five minutes for her to walk to our house, and she could come over whenever she wanted.

When I said this, the two Kenyan men I was speaking with let out offended hisses. They explained to me that in their culture a man must keep his distance from his mother-in-law. It would be very offensive if she were ever to show up at his house. The man's wife was free to travel to her mother's house, but the mother-in-law would never spend the night at her daughter's house. Needless to say, mother-in-law apartments don't increase resale value in Kenya!

Is our American cultural practice better than this Kenyan practice? No, not at all. In fact, some Americans may wish they could be more like Kenyans in this particular area! But my point is that something very normal to an American can be incredibly offensive to someone from another culture.

These cultural norms influence how we read our Bibles. Those parts of the Bible that we want to dismiss or water down because they are offensive might be easily accepted by other cultures. Meanwhile a different culture may have a variant set of teachings in the Bible they try to explain away. Who is right?

Both cultures probably have blind spots. We need each other to help interpret Scripture. And that is the problem when we say, "My only creed is the Bible." You are separating yourself from all other believers, who have different perspectives and can see your blind spots better than you do.

A Local Church Determines Essential Doctrine

Another common option is for a church to define what the correct doctrine is. This could be anything from a single, independent church with a statement of beliefs to something like the LDS Church where there is a prophet who controls what the key doctrines are. Some denominations or church associations would fall into this category as well. In this system, a select group of people get to define what is essential doctrine. Many churches function just fine in this system, but, as we will see in the next section, that is because they aren't truly letting that church alone define doctrine.

This approach also has weaknesses. Some of the weaknesses of the individually-defined correct doctrine apply here as well. Take for instance a new non-denominational church in suburban Utah that comes up with its own doctrinal statement. Simply because of the demographics of that place, the main people constructing the doctrinal statement will likely be upper-middle-class white people. This isn't inherently bad, but their reading of Scripture will be influenced by the fact that they all come from a similar culture.

When church doctrine is controlled by a single person or a select group of people, what checks and balances are there? What's to keep the leaders from straying from Scripture to meet their own needs to try to perpetuate their own organization? What power do individuals in the church have to hold the leaders accountable? Are they simply subject to the whims of the leadership? Fortunately, most church leaders want to do the right thing, but this structure does make abuse of power easier.

Church Creeds Determine Essential Doctrine

This final category where we look at creeds is the one most likely to cause people to break out in hives! But I'd ask you to give this scary idea a chance, because it is quite valuable to the Church.

We've identified two main difficulties in coming up with the essential doctrines of the Church. First, we are bound up by our own cultural blind spots. Second, those in power can use that power for their own good instead of the good of the people they are supposed to serve.

We need something that spans cultural boundaries, something that we can appeal to as an independent authority, something that even those in power can be held accountable to. Creeds do just this.

People today may want to disparage creeds, for they were written by a bunch of old, dead men. But perhaps that is our cultural bias speaking. Other cultures give great weight to what those before them have said.

Creeds are documents that have been tested over and over again. They span generations and cross cultural borders. Christians from Africa to Asia and the Western world have said yes, we believe these things. The multicultural and multi-generational acceptance of these historic creeds show that although the creeds were originally written by a small group of people, they have transcended their original audience and spoken to the world.

It is possible for a church today to come up with a doctrinal statement that becomes one of the classic statements of the faith, but only time will tell. The benefit of these historic creeds is that time has proved these documents to be accurate representations of the basics of Christian faith.

Take for example the Apostles' Creed. This creed was widely accepted in the fourth century as a summary of basic Christian belief. It's important to note that a creed is not an addition to Scripture. It sits underneath Scripture and should be corrected whenever it is found to stray from the Bible. A creed's purpose is to state essential doctrines, not to tell us something the Bible doesn't teach. You could think of it as the CliffsNotes version of Scripture.

Everyone has some creed. The person who says, "No creed but the Bible," has just stated her creed. The Church that comes up with a statement of beliefs has just written its own creed. So the question is, what creed will you use?

It's pretty bold to think that your personal statement of beliefs is better than something that has lasted two thousand years. Is it likely that a statement of beliefs written by a single church is better than something that millions of Christians have deemed a good summary of beliefs? When an individual or a local church develops a new creed, that local body is in control of the creed not subject to it.

Part of the value of these historic creeds is that even church leadership must be subject to them. So if a pastor decides he wants to change his belief on who Jesus was, any person in that congregation, even a child, would have the right to challenge the pastor based on the authority of this creed (remember the creed is simply a summary of essential Christian beliefs). The creed helps us know that it's not worth calling your pastor out on wearing blended wool clothing, but it is worth calling him out on preaching that Jesus is not God's only son.

The value of these creeds becomes clearer when we see how they allow churches in various denominations to enjoy fellowship. Instead of having to explain all the nuances of what you believe, you can simply say, "I believe what is taught in the Apostles' Creed." While no creed is perfect, they do help people recognize if they share essential beliefs.

If someone moves from a Methodist church to a Presbyterian church, he is moving between two churches that hold to the Apostles' Creed. Changing churches does not change whether she is Christian or not. She is simply moving around in the family of Christ's Church. They would not need to be re-baptized or prove they are Christian in some other way.

Is this use of creeds biblical? Perhaps this is a harder case to make, but we get some indication that creed-like structures were appearing even during the apostles' time. Colossians 1:15–20 is seen as an early form of a creed concerning Christ. Paul writes:

> *The Son is the image of the invisible God, the firstborn over all creation. For in him all things were created: things in heaven and on earth, visible and invisible, whether thrones or powers or rulers or authorities; all things have been created through him and for him. He is before all things, and in him all things hold together. And he is the head of the body, the church; he is the beginning and the firstborn from among the dead, so that in everything he might have the supremacy. For God was pleased to have all his fullness dwell in him, and through him to reconcile to himself all things, whether things on earth or things in heaven, by making peace through his blood, shed on the cross.*

In 2 Timothy, Paul instructs Timothy in how the Church should continue after the age of the apostles. He says, *"Follow the pattern of the sound words that you have heard from me, in the faith and love that are in Christ Jesus. By the Holy Spirit who dwells within us, guard the good deposit entrusted to you"* (2 Tim 1:13–14, ESV). Paul here seems to be speaking of something other than Scripture as a whole. His use of the word "pattern" (not just "sound words") indicates that he may be talking about a creedal statement. In fact, in the preceding verses (2 Tim 1:9–10), Paul gives Timothy a pattern of words summarizing Christian doctrine. Paul is commending Timothy to pass this pattern of words (a creed) along with Scripture on to future generations.

The three most widely used creeds are the Apostles', Nicene, and Athanasian, which can all easily be found online. These creeds have been used for centuries and across cultures and denominations. When a church holds to these creeds, it makes it easier to know if they hold to the basic teachings of Christianity. I've included the texts of these common creeds in Appendix 2.

Confessions of Faith

At one level, the creeds may be underwhelming because of all they *don't* mention. They tend to focus a lot on the person of Christ and his work. This simplicity reminds us of the beauty of the Gospel. Our salvation is not based on our ability to understand complex doctrine. It's not even based on our ability to get all our doctrine correct! No, the assurance for our salvation is found in the person and work of Christ. It is God who saves us, not ourselves or our doctrines.

However, this doesn't mean there is no need for working out our beliefs in greater detail. If we love God, then we should want to know as much about him as possible. We should want to live our lives in a way that is most pleasing to him.

Thus, once we are to move beyond creeds as the lowest common denominator, we arrive at confessions of faith. These are more robust documents that spell out many more doctrinal details. For example, the Westminster Confession of Faith outlines the beliefs of the denomination where I am a pastor. Some Baptists hold to the Baptist Confession of 1689, which was based on the Westminster Confession but updated to reflect important distinctions that Baptists hold. These documents have some of the same benefits of creeds. They have transcended individual denominations, times, and cultures and thus have the weight of the Church behind them.

But they don't carry the same weight as these creeds. To deny the Apostles' Creed would mean you were not a Christian. But to deny the Westminster Confession of Faith would simply mean you weren't Presbyterian. Confessions of faith are helpful in understanding the theological differences between particular denominations and churches. If a church simply says, "We hold to the Baptist Confession of Faith," that gives you a good idea of its theological convictions.

Summary

While different church denominations may have many outward differences, all true Christian churches agree on the basics of the faith. Worship styles or particular denominational affiliations are much less important than holding to the time-tested basics of the Christian faith.

One helpful way to understand these differences is through this diagram:

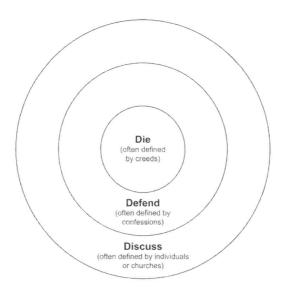

This diagram summarizes much of what we've talked about so far. The DIE circle encompasses those beliefs that are essential to Christianity—those beliefs that we would die for. As we have discussed, the historic creeds summarize these essential beliefs. The seven points of unity (Paul's seven "one"s) in Ephesians 4 make up this list. Any church that holds to these basics is part of God's one Church. Any person who holds to these beliefs is a brother or sister in the Lord. It doesn't matter what other label one may have.

The DEFEND circle is often what makes up the differences in denominations. Confessional documents usually outline these beliefs. For example, one might not agree with everything in the Westminster Confession of Faith but still be a true Christian. Issues around baptizing infants, the end times, or forms of church government would fit in this sphere.

The DISCUSS circle is the most loosely held set of beliefs. The items in this sphere are influenced by personal preferences, various cultures, and other more subjective factors. These items should play a lesser role in deciding upon a church. If you find a church where all your "discuss" items match up, just wait a little longer! You'll be sure to find some places where you disagree. If a particular belief is not mentioned in the historic creeds or the widely accepted confessions of faith, then there is a good chance it's a belief that fits into this category.

I recently saw a satirical news article titled, "Unsatisfied Persecuted Church Member to Try Out Other Church Just across Minefield."[4] This man in Iraq will be taking his family eight hours across a minefield to a different church because he's not really connecting with his current one. The article pokes fun at the consumer mentality so many of us have when picking a church.

Because we have access to so many churches, many of us have let those items in the "discuss" circle become the most important. But instead, as we are reminded what it costs our brothers and sisters to attend any church at all, we should be thankful to find any church where we agree with the items in the "die" circle. Furthermore, when we start focusing on those things that unite us as believers, our preferences will become less important.

We will realize that the most important thing is our

unity in Christ. We are all sinners. We all need grace. We are all on a journey to know Christ. Therefore, even if we don't feel like we have much in common with the people in a church, or it doesn't match all of our preferences, we do have Christ in common. He is big enough to cover over our differences.

DIVERSITY OF CHURCHES

The questions that often arise after talking about unity include, "Why then are there so many churches? If there is one God and one truth, why not just one denomination, or Church?" These are great questions, and they lead us into my favorite part of this book.

I believe there is a biblical basis for a diversity of churches that finds its foundation in God himself. In other words, when done correctly, the abundance of different churches is not something to lament. It is something to celebrate, because there is diversity in God himself. If God cannot be captured in one single person but requires three different persons to be God, then certainly no one church (or even denomination) could hope to capture or to reflect all the diversity and complexity of God. Let's look at the biblical basis for this argument.

When people ask me why there are so many churches, I often respond, "Why are there four Gospels?"

Few people have given this much thought. But then they realize each Gospel account gives us a different, unique glimpse or aspect of Jesus and his ministry.

Imagine what we might miss if we didn't have one of the Gospels. If we didn't have the Gospel of Matthew, our children wouldn't be able to dress up like wise men for the Christmas play. And we'd never sing "We Three Kings." Wait, did Matthew actually say there were three kings? I'll let you figure that out!

If we didn't have Luke, we would never know of the angels' announcement to the shepherds of Jesus's birth. The Christmas classic "Hark the Herald Angels Sing" would never have been written. Imagine how different our Christmas traditions would be if we were missing just one Gospel!

Now, conversely if we did just have one Gospel, could you know enough about Jesus to be saved? Certainly many have come to faith by reading only the short Gospel of Mark. But having four Gospel accounts gives us a rich, four-dimensional, eyewitness picture of Jesus and his ministry. We gain the great blessing of a diversity of accounts all unified in the same core message of who Jesus is and what he did.

I've found it helpful to think about God's truth like a large mountain. In Salt Lake City, we are very familiar with how the Wasatch Mountains look from the west. But if you look at those same mountains from the east, they look very different. Now imagine four people, each looking at the same mountain from a different direction. Each person describes the same mountain, but because of the complexity and diversity of each side, their descriptions will sound different.

Similarly each Gospel describes Jesus' ministry from a different vantage point, but they are all describing the same Jesus. Each account helps us to get to know Jesus a little better. And because each one of us comes from a different place, we might find that we resonate with one account more than the others.

God gave us the Bible with four Gospels, four different perspectives. Therefore, he wants us to have a four-dimensional picture of Jesus.[1]

Diversity in God Himself

Let's now take this discussion about diversity one step further. Consider the historic view of God as a Trinity. The Westminster Shorter Catechism gives us a helpful definition of the Trinity:

> There are three persons in the Godhead; the Father, the Son, and the Holy Ghost; and these three are one God, the same in substance, equal in power and glory.

While the term "Trinity" is not found in the Bible, it is simply a word used to describe how Scripture speaks of the three persons (Father, Son, and Spirit) in the Godhead as one God. We see this in how the Gospel of John describes the relationship between Jesus and God, *"and the Word was with God, and the Word was God"* (John 1:1). John later tells us that the Word is Jesus. How do you reconcile what John says? That Jesus was *with* God implies separateness, while his next statement that Jesus *was* God[2] implies unity. The term "Trinity" is an attempt to capture the paradox in John's statement. Jesus is separate from God, but Jesus is God. Thus we say there are three persons making up one God. That's the Trinity.

This is a key definition of God. It is crucial for our discussion about diversity because it shows that diversity finds its foundation in God himself. God is diverse! God is three unique persons! Thus the diversity we see in people and churches is something that actually is a reflection of God's own nature.

Now, consider if God were not a Trinity. Salvation would, in fact, not be possible. Each person in the Godhead has a role to play in salvation. God the Father chose us before the foundation of the world and predestined us to be his children through Jesus Christ (Eph 1:3–6). Jesus Christ works to accomplish forgiveness, redemption, and adoption through his blood (Eph 1:7–12). The Holy Spirit applies the work of salvation into our lives and acts as a downpayment of God's promise to bring us home to him (Eph 1:13–14).

If one person of the Trinity is removed, salvation breaks apart. If Jesus were not equal with God, could he provide a worthy sacrifice for the sins of the world? If God is just one person playing different roles, then when Jesus died, God died. Something dead cannot come back to life without something outside bringing that life. If there is no Trinity, how did Jesus come back to life? If

Jesus did not fully die, can we have any assurance that the full penalty for our sins has been paid?

If you remove one person from the Godhead, it ceases to be God. In other words, diversity is required for God to be God.

Now, let's make the jump to the Church in the world. As people called to reflect God, should we not also reflect that diversity that finds its foundation in God himself? Again, we are not talking about core theological beliefs, but about our various perspectives as denominations and churches. Some churches, because of their history or background, will be great at missions, while other churches may be better at teaching, and still others may excel at mercy ministries. But because we are finite, no one church could do all these things perfectly.

The Apostle Paul makes a similar argument in 1 Corinthians 12:12–31. He first talks about the diversity we have in the Church; people come from different ethnicities, backgrounds, economic classes, etc. But he also says we are unified because *"we have all been baptized into one body by one Spirit, and we all share the same Spirit"* (1 Cor 12:13b, New Living Translation).

Paul compares the Church to a human body. A body has many different parts. The foot doesn't look like the ear, and the ear doesn't look like the hand. And each part plays a different role.

But even though they are different, they are still part of the same body. They need to work together. Paul then takes his analogy a step further and says, *"How strange a body would be if it had only one part"* (1 Cor 12:19). Paul is arguing that diversity is required for the Church to be the Church.

Now, we often think about this passage in terms of a particular, local church. And certainly this is a valid application. But consider what defines the one body. Paul answers that in 1 Corinthians 12:13 when he says, *"But we have all been baptized into one body by one Spirit."* This means Paul is primarily talking about the one true Church, which exists throughout time and space.

Therefore, various churches and even denominations will act like certain body parts. A particular church may have a culture or history that lends itself to be better at one thing over another. Some churches excel at teaching the great truths of the Christian faith. Other churches are really good at taking care of each other and making sure there isn't anyone in need within the Church. Still other churches have fruitful ministries that excel at caring for their neighborhoods and cities. All these are important parts of what the church should do. But no one church is able to do it all.

God does not call us to create one single megachurch or denomination. Paul has shown us that there is already one Church, made up of all who were baptized into the one body. God calls us to celebrate the diversity of our gifts and work together as the one body of Christ.

Denominations

Perhaps one of the more confusing things about looking for a church is understanding denominational labels. You can visit two Baptist churches, and the worship services may feel completely different. You can visit two Presbyterian churches that have opposite theological convictions. For the uninitiated, this can be overwhelming and even depressing.

Denominational titles can tell us two different things: the form of church government and the theological beliefs. Words like "Presbyterian" and "Baptist" will tell us what form of government the church has. But we must also ask, "What kind of Presbyterian is this church?" A church in the Presbyterian Church in America (PCA) is different than one from the Presbyterian Church (PCUSA). Both use a Presbyterian form of government, but they hold different theological positions on some matters.

Forms of Church Government

Most churches fall under one of three forms of government.

Congregational

The authority of the local church lies within the members of the congregation. Decisions are made through business meetings where each member of the congregation gets to vote. The church may be part of a denomination, but the authority resides in the local church.

Examples: Baptist   churches,   Congregational churches.

Presbyterian

The authority of the local church lies within a group of elders of that church. These elders are elected by the congregation. While each member of the congregation has a vote in major church decisions like hiring the pastor or buying land, the elders hold the main authority. The denomination as a whole is governed by the elders of the Presbyterian churches, not by any one person.

Examples: Presbyterian   churches,   Christian Reformed churches, Reformed Church in America.

Episcopal

This is the most hierarchical form of government. Authority is found in a single bishop who oversees the whole denomination. Decisions made at the top trickle down to all the congregations. The individuals have no real power over the church.

Examples: Catholic churches, Episcopal churches, Methodist churches, some Lutheran churches, Some non-denominational churches would effectively operate this way at the local church level.

Why Are There So Many Denominations?

There are many reasons why there are so many denominations, but most denominations were founded because of political or theological reasons.

Political

The Reformation in Europe led to denominations separating along country lines. In the US, the Civil War saw denominations split across North/South lines.

Geographical

As European immigrants entered into the United States, it was impractical to maintain denominational ties with the churches in Europe. Thus new denominations were created to provide oversight for newly created immigrant churches in the United State. These churches often first held worship services in the native language of the immigrants and served an important role to help new immigrants get connected in the community.

Theological

Starting in the 1900s, major denominations in the US faced what was called the fundamentalist-modernist controversy. This controversy centered around central theological issues, like one's view on the authority and accuracy of Scripture. This led to the splitting of most denominations in the US along theological lines. This is why two Presbyterian churches can have different theologies.

The Authority of Scripture and Denominations

A denomination's (or church's) view of Scripture is important in choosing a church. I don't believe it is necessary to hold to the inerrancy of the Scriptures in order to be considered a Christian. However, I think the inerrancy of the Scriptures is incredibly important, and holding to it has tremendous implications for people, churches, and denominations.

Inerrancy means "without error." Inerrancy, infallibility, and inspiration are terms used to describe the authority of Scripture. Inspiration means Scripture words are God's words. Inerrancy and infallibility are terms used to say Scripture contains no errors in what God seeks to communicate.

The concept called "the inspiration of Scripture" is a term referring to how Paul describes all Scripture as "God-breathed" in 2 Timothy 3:16. Paul means that the words of Scripture are words breathed out by God through human authors.

A belief in the inspiration of Scripture provides a crucial safeguard to the Bible and its interpretation. If you don't hold to the inerrancy of Scripture, the Bible can then become a tool to further one's own agenda. Isolated Scripture passages could be used to justify just about anything. If we believe all Scripture ultimately came from God, we must believe there is a limit to what interpretations are valid, namely those which were intended by God himself. Any interpretation must be in agreement with the whole of Scripture. Anything less than inspiration by God makes it impossible to refute poor interpretations and misused Scriptures. Only an inerrant text has the exact words God desired to be written in the original manuscripts.

The idea of inspiration has often been misunderstood. Critics have used apparent contradictions in Scripture or the clear marks of the human author to disprove its inspiration. On the other hand, some believe the human author is simply a mannequin through whom God dictated his words. But neither of these positions reflect a proper understanding of inspiration. In his essay "How Does the Bible Look at Itself?" Sinclair Ferguson sums up what inspiration means with three points: 1) Scripture bears witness to its character as God's inspired word; 2) Scripture is the written form of God's word; and 3) Scripture bears the marks of its human authors. God used human authors to write his message as he intended it to be written.

Attending a church that holds to the inspiration of Scripture gives you the comfort of knowing what that church's authority is. While our interpretation of Scripture is not always perfect, when our objective standard is inspired Scripture, we can all hold one another accountable to that. When a church or denomination does not have this objective standard, it may not be clear what their authority actually is. Every one of us subscribes to some authority, whether we realize it or not (society's rules, tradition, our conscience). If a church does not believe Scripture to be its highest authority, it is not resting on a solid foundation.

What About Non-denominational Churches?

The past thirty years have seen an explosion in non-denominational churches. One advantage of a denominational title is that it allows you to quickly know where a church stands on a wide variety of issues. Because a non-denominational church is by definition not connected to a denomination, it can be more difficult to understand what it believes. Many of these churches have statements of faith on their websites. This will certainly provide some help, but won't be as helpful as adherence to a historic confession. Most non-denominational churches would be considered evangelical. "Evangelical" is an umbrella term (not a denomination) used to describe churches that hold to the authority of the Bible, the need for conversion, and trust in Jesus' saving work. In addition to most non-denominational churches, many churches within denominations are also evangelical.

Summary

We've looked at a lot regarding the unity and diversity of churches. But one thing we didn't look at was the different theological beliefs among various denominations and churches. For instance, some churches baptize babies, while some only baptize those who can make a profession of faith. Some churches hold to a Calvinist theology, others an Arminian one. The list could go on, and it can get overwhelming quickly. This is where the historic creeds (and the internet!) are useful. They help us know what are the important parts of Christian doctrine and what are areas where we can disagree yet still have Christian fellowship. Thus so many of the theological differences between various churches and denominations are more like family disagreements. We are all part of the same family, the household of God. This is not to minimize the importance of studying theology. However, people's theology develops over time. As you read Scripture and Christian books and talk with others, your theology will develop and you will begin to understand where you fall on certain issues. Be willing to change your mind. But those issues are peripheral. They do not make you Christian or not. Finding a church that holds to the basics of the faith is of first importance.

4

WORSHIP EXPLAINED

When we think of worship we tend to think of something religious people do. Christians worship on Sundays. Jews observe the Sabbath on Saturday. Muslims gather for worship on Friday. But does that mean worship is restricted to only religious people? Not at all. Everyone worships.

Webster's dictionary says that worship is "extravagant respect or admiration for or devotion to an object of esteem." Using that definition, we can see how worship happens at sports events, concerts, movies, and more. Scripture teaches this same thing in Romans 1:25. It says that instead of worshiping God, we worship and serve created things rather than the Creator. So when Christians worship, we are doing something that is natural. What is different is the *object* of our worship. Instead of worshiping created things, we worship the Creator.

But it won't take long to realize there can be big differences in a worship service from one church to another. You may find that a certain style of worship is more comfortable to you. For some, the presence of drums and guitars is a big adjustment they struggle to get used to. Others find such styles of worship invigorating and refreshing. They don't want hymns or organs. The good news is that a biblical church can have bands on a stage or just a piano and hymn book.

We all have preferences, and these can change over time, stage of life, and other factors in the church. We should make sure that whatever style a church uses, it is worshiping in accordance with God's intent.

Organ Versus Rock Band

After a church's doctrinal beliefs, worship style is one of the most influential factors in finding a church. Most denominations allow flexibility in the style of worship a church uses, so don't assume that all Presbyterian or Baptist worship services are the same.

We all have preferences in styles, but don't fall into the trap that traditional worship means boring and contemporary worship means exciting. I have seen churches that sing only hymns with more gusto and spirit than churches with rock bands. More important than any particular style is the question, "Does our worship reflect the glory of God?" The answer can be "yes" for both the contemporary and the traditional worship services.

Revelation 5 helpfully illumines this. In a picture of heaven, God is seated on his throne and holding a scroll with seven seals. A call goes out asking who is worthy to open the sealed scroll. Initially, it looks as if no one is worthy. But then a lamb that looks like it has been slain comes to the throne and opens the sacred scroll. This is Jesus, the Lamb of God, the only one worthy to open the sacred scroll. Many creatures are watching this. What is their response when they witness this? They fall down and worship. They shout out in praise:

> *You are worthy to take the scroll*
> > *and to open its seals,*
> > *because you were slain,*
> > *and with your blood you purchased for God*
> > *persons from every tribe and language and people*
> *and nation.*
> > *You have made them to be a kingdom and priests to*
> *serve our God,*
> > *and they will reign on the earth.* (Rev 5:9–10)

When people behold the glory of and wonder of Jesus, the natural reaction is to worship. It's an impulse.

We get this when we are struck by the beauty of a sunset. The picture of Jesus in Revelation 5 is like the beauty of a thousand sunsets. When people see this, they cannot help but be overcome and respond in worship.

That is the ideal worship we will experience in heaven. While our worship on earth will never rise to that level, what can we expect? What should we strive for? Let's turn to Hebrews.

> *But you have come to Mount Zion, to the city of the*

living God, the heavenly Jerusalem. You have come to thousands upon thousands of angels in joyful assembly, to the church of the firstborn, whose names are written in heaven. You have come to God, the Judge of all, to the spirits of the righteous made perfect, to Jesus the mediator of a new covenant, and to the sprinkled blood that speaks a better word than the blood of Abel. (Heb 12:22–24)

This passage is talking about God's people assembling for worship, and it is remarkable. When God's people gather together for worship, they are, in a spiritual sense, gathering with all of God's people before his throne! There are many similarities here between worship on earth and the pictures of ideal worship in heaven. There is a large crowd filled with all God's people and angels. We surround God's throne, where God and Jesus are present. One could easily mistake this passage from Hebrews for a description of heaven. But this is what happens through our union with Christ in his spirit when we gather for worship in this life!

So how do we access such heavenly worship? Let's look at the elements of a worship service.

The Elements of a Worship Service

The picture God gives us of worship is breathtaking! Everything is centered around God and adoring his beauty. In worship we are light-reflectors of God's glory making him shine even brighter.

But if worship is all about God does this mean there are no benefits for us? Certainly not! In fact although worship's focus is fully on God, when we participate in worship it changes us. It makes us look more like the one we worship. But because God is at the center of worship, we must do it in the way he prescribes. In other words, if we worship in ways that we like without care for if that worship falls in line with how God wants us to worship, we won't experience the benefits of life-changing worship.

Perhaps this sounds a bit odd, but consider this illustration. Recently I installed a new thermostat in our house. It was important to correctly match up the wires that come from our furnace and air conditioner to the new thermostat. If I simply connected the wires however I wanted, I may be in for a surprise when I wanted A/C and the heat came on because I had mixed up the wires. This would be incredibly frustrating because I wouldn't get any of the benefits of central cooling and heating.

It's the same with worship. God gives us specific instructions for plugging in the wires so that we receive the benefits in worship he has intended. If we just worship however we like or however makes us feel good, we will feel the consequences. We haven't connected the wires in accordance with God's design.

The Bible is full of examples of people worshiping God outside of the ways he has commanded (see Lev 10:1–3 and 1 Sam 15:22 for two examples). We could summarize God's intent in Jesus' conversation with the

Samaritan woman at the well when he tells her that we
must worship God in spirit and truth (John 4:20:26).

Let's then look at the elements God has given us to
plug into his blessings in worship.[1]

Preach the Word

God uses preaching to deliver his unchanging word
to our changing world. It is through preaching that
people grow towards maturity in Christ (1 Cor 2:1–4,
Col 1:28–29, 2 Tim 4:1–3).

Read the Word

Scripture is God's letter to his people. Thus we
should hear his word read. It is useful for teaching and
training in righteousness. Paul regularly gives instructions for Scripture to be read in the churches (1 Tim
4:13, Col 4:16, 1 Thess 5:27).

Sing the Word

Singing is a part of worship in both the Old Testament and New Testament. It has both vertical (praise to
God) and horizontal (encouragement to one another)
dimensions (Col 3:16, Eph 5:18–19).

Pray the Word

Prayer is our way of communicating with God. Paul commands corporate prayer among all people (1 Tim 2:1–8). When the church prays corporately it shows unity in Christ and also learns to pray through hearing the prayers of the elders.

See the Word

People often want visual elements in worship. God has given us his sacraments as ways for us to see (and feel, taste, smell, etc.) his Word to us. The Lord's Supper and Baptism are to be parts of our worship (Matt 28:19–20, 1 Cor 11:23–26).

Because God cares how we worship—in spirit and truth—you need to make sure you are asking questions beyond, "Do I like this particular church's worship?" You should ensure that a particular church's worship falls in line with God's intent. The following questions can help you do that.

Does the Worship Put God at the Center?

Our word "worship" comes from an Old English word that means "to acknowledge the worth of something." When you rave about the latest movie you saw, that's worship. When you drool over that new sports car, that's worship. Worship is saying that something is worthy of praise.

Therefore the worship service is the acknowledgement of the worth of God. Thus each element of the service must put God at the center. The end of the service should leave us thinking more highly of God. Did the worship service you attended do that?

Does the Worship Connect Us with Other Churches?

As we have already seen, the Church as a whole is connected through the Spirit. Our worship should remind us of this connection, that we are not alone. There are millions of other Christians past, present, and future with whom we participate in worship. Does the service remind us of our connection to these other churches? Is the church using only the newest and coolest songs, or do we also sing songs that other Christians around the globe have sung? Are there elements of worship that remind us of our unity with other churches? While reciting a creed is not popular today, such an act connects us with Christians who have recited those creeds for the past 1,600 years. It reminds us that we are not creating something new, but standing in a long tradition of people who have come before us.

Are the Songs Singable?

Paul said we should be *"admonishing one another in all wisdom, singing psalms and hymns and spiritual songs"* (Col 3:16, ESV). God is the object of the worship, but we are the benefactors of worship. When we sing, we sing to God, but also to each other for mutual encouragement. We sing for the benefit of others. Some of you may say that not-singing brings more edification than if you were to sing! But when we all sing together, no matter how good or bad our voices are, it shows that we are all part of one another. Our voices blend so that we all sound good together.

Are the worship songs singable? Sometimes we use tunes or styles that are so archaic that we have trouble singing them. In other places, the worship feels so much like a concert that no one else can follow along with the performance on stage.

The Sermon: Why Do Pastors Like to Talk So Much?

In most Protestant services, the sermon holds an important place. But sermons can take various forms. I've heard of a pastor who gave part of his sermon while hanging from a wire above the stage, mimicking the angels that announced the birth of Jesus to shepherds. Other pastors will simply walk up to the pulpit and read from typed pages in a monotone voice. Let's take a moment to look at why pastors preach, how to know if a sermon is good, and what different types of sermons you may encounter.

Why Preach at All?

In our multimedia world, preaching seems drastically out of touch. And indeed many churches have altered the format of sermons to include other forms of media. Other churches have eschewed preaching altogether. I've often heard a quote (mis-) attributed to St. Francis of Assisi,

"Preach the Gospel; use words if necessary." Should you care if there is preaching at a church?

While preaching may seem out of date, I would argue that people hear preaching every single day. Thus Christian preaching is all the more necessary. While we don't see people gathering to sit and hear someone talk like we did in days past, everyone still hears all kinds of preaching. My two-year-old daughter knows all the lyrics to the song from *Frozen,* "Let It Go." It's cute to hear her sing the words, but it's also a bit alarming. "Let It Go" has a subtle message, and it influences how we think. A sermon could be thought of as any public statement intending to convey a message. "Let Is Go" is a sermon proclaiming that in order to be truly fulfilled, we must no longer conceal what is inside us, but "let it go." Only then will we be truly happy.

"Let It Go" is a subtle form of preaching. Every day, through the TV shows we watch and the songs we hear, we are being preached to. The messages are influencing us, often without us noticing.

Now, before you get paranoid and want to throw away all your iPads, you should realize that this type of thing has been happening since the birth of the Church. When Paul and Barnabas were traveling on their missionary journey, they visited a town called Iconium. As Paul and Barnabas were speaking about the gospel, a group of Jews who did not like this message *"poisoned [the people's] minds against [Paul and Barnabas]"* (Acts 14:2). Later in the chapter we see this same crowd do it again. From the beginning of the Church, people have tried to alter the Gospel and convince others not to believe it.

Simply by living in this world, you will hear and be influenced by all kinds of preaching. What is the solution to weathering this influence? It's biblical preaching.

Biblical preaching is God's solution to the constant bombardment of messages that turn us toward other things. Paul, in some of his final words to his student Timothy, makes the importance of preaching very clear:

> *In the presence of God and of Christ Jesus, who will judge the living and the dead, and in view of his appearing and his kingdom, I give you this charge: Preach the word; be prepared in season and out of season; correct, rebuke and encourage—with great patience and careful instruction. For the time will come when people will not put up with sound doctrine. Instead, to suit their own desires, they will gather around them a great number of teachers to say what their itching ears want to hear. (2 Tim 4:1–3)*

What does Paul tell Timothy is vitally important, especially when people are being heavily influenced by their culture? The preaching of God's word.

Why does God give us preaching to preserve and grow his Church? Romans 10:17 tells us, *"So faith comes from hearing, that is, hearing the Good News about Christ"* (New Living Translation). And what is the importance of faith? Ephesians 2:8 says, *"For it is by grace you have been saved, through faith"* (NIV). Faith is the pipeline that connects us to God's unending grace. Without hearing the good news about Christ, we will never have that pipeline. Thus preaching is of utmost importance. A church that does not take it seriously does it to the detriment of everyone present.

Preaching Is Miraculous

But is Christian preaching simply a way to counter the erroneous messages we are bombarded with? No! Christian preaching is miraculous. It brings new life, because it plays a vital role in God's work of making a new creation, one where the world is as it ought to be. This seems like a tall order for the person who gets up each week to speak. The good news is that the power of preaching doesn't come from the speaker; it comes from God and his word.

In order to see the miraculous power of words we only need to look to Genesis 1 where God creates the world. God speaks, and darkness gives way to light. God speaks, and deserts become lush gardens. God speaks, and stuff happens!

Not long after the creation of the world, sin entered the picture. It messed up life as it was supposed to be. It broke the relationship between God his people. But God promised he would make all things new again. He would begin a work of new creation, to restore and redeem everything that was broken. He would do this in Christ, and that new-creation work would spread to everyone who believed in Christ and eventually overtake the whole world (Eph 1:3–10).

How then does this work of making all things new spread throughout the world? It's by preaching. God takes the preacher's ordinary words and imbues them with his holy power (1 Cor 2:1–5).

Ezekiel 37 gives us an incredible picture of this power. God takes the prophet Ezekiel to a valley filled with dry bones. The vultures had gotten their fill. Maggots and worms finished the job. And now the desert sun had bleached the remaining bones until they started to crack. God then asked Ezekiel if these bones could live. Ezekiel responds by saying, *"O Lord God, you know"* (Ez 37:3). God tells Ezekiel to speak to the bones, *"O dry bones, hear the word of the Lord"* (Ez 37:4).

As Ezekiel did so, the bones started coming together. Flesh appeared, oxygen filled their lungs, and suddenly from the dry bones sprang up an army of living people!

That is the power of God's word. Preaching in this biblical sense matters because it's how God works in the world to bring life out of death. Preaching can occur behind a pulpit or in a valley of dry bones. The location doesn't matter. Preaching is what God uses to restore life to what has died.

How Do I Evaluate a Sermon?

While there are many preferences for sermons, only one question matters: Is Jesus Christ proclaimed? The Apostle Paul sums this up in Colossians 1:27–29:

> *To them God chose to make known how great among*

the Gentiles are the riches of the glory of this mystery,
which is Christ in you, the hope of glory. Him we
proclaim, warning everyone and teaching everyone
with all wisdom, that we may present everyone mature
in Christ. For this I toil, struggling with all his energy
that he powerfully works within me. (ESV)

Verse 29 tells us that *for this* he focuses all his energy. *This* is proclaiming Christ. A sermon is successful if Christ is proclaimed. A sermon has failed if Christ is not proclaimed.

Why is this so important? Because Christ in us is a rich source of power for believers. Proclaiming Christ in us changes the believer from the inside out, so that he or she will become mature in Christ. For those who do not know Christ, he is the power unto salvation. Both the believer and nonbeliever need Christ proclaimed. It is how they come to know God's grace, and it is how they come to grow in that grace. Every week, everyone needs Christ proclaimed. This is why Paul labored with all his energy to always preach Christ. So while we all may have preferences for a pastor's speech or style, one thing must be present, and that is that Christ is proclaimed.

Some argue that if we preach Christ every week, we could get bored of hearing the same thing, and shouldn't mature Christians be dealing with deeper things? Others argue it's not really practical. For instance, what does Christ proclaimed have to do with helping me raise kids?

First, just because Christ is proclaimed every week, it doesn't mean the message is the same every week. We just need to look at Scripture to see that. In Luke 24:44–46, the resurrected Jesus is speaking to his disciples, and he says *"that everything written about me in the Law of Moses and the Prophets and the Psalms must be fulfilled."*

During this time "the Law, Prophets, and Psalms" was a shorthand for describing all the Old Testament as we know it today. Jesus is saying that every part of Scripture speaks about him. The next verse says, *"Then he opened their minds to understand the Scriptures."* Notice it doesn't say he opened their eyes to understand part of the Old Testament. Nor does it say he opened their eyes to understand just the parts of Scripture that speak explicitly about him. But every part of the Old Testament speaks of Christ.

In Luke 24:46–47 Jesus summarizes the message of the Old Testament, *"Thus it is written, that the Christ should suffer and on the third day rise from the dead, and that repentance and forgiveness of sins should be proclaimed in his name to all nations, beginning from Jerusalem."* This sounds like something out of the New Testament, but the New Testament had not yet been written. Jesus is saying this is the message of the Old Testament! In other words from Genesis 1 to Malachi, every part of Scripture teaches us about Christ. Therefore, just because we are called to preach Christ all the time it doesn't mean the message will be exactly the same, for there are sixty-six books of Scripture from which we can preach Christ.

But what about the practicality of preaching Christ every week? What does that have to do with helping me in my work or in raising kids? The short answer is *everything*!

Take work for example. Many of us work for the weekends. Work frustrations can cause us to dread Mondays. In Genesis 1 and 2, we learn that God created humans to work, but work in the Garden of Eden was fulfilling and joyful because there was no opposition or friction. In fact, our work of creating things—farming, or construction or computer programming—mimics our Heavenly Father as the first creator. But in Genesis 3, sin breaks into the world, and work (though still necessary) becomes a difficult chore. What hope is there to find meaning in our work?

Let me give you a personal example. I often seek to find my worth in what I do. If I'm succeeding in my work, I think I have worth. If I'm not, I can feel like a failure. I'm often driven to be successful because I believe that will give me more worth. I can feel this temptation in my work as a pastor, but I also feel it elsewhere.

I love riding my bicycle in the mountains of Utah. But I've learned one of the reasons I like pushing myself on my bike is because I believe that the faster I am compared to others, the more worth I have. Perhaps that sounds silly, and it is! But it's also the way my sinful heart works.

So what's the solution? It's ultimately the Gospel. Nothing else will truly change me.

So how does the Gospel speak to this struggle? Here are a few ways:

- The Gospel shows me that nothing I do will ever be enough. I've learned my successes fade quickly. They have a short shelf life. Soon I'm yearning for something different to give me a renewed sense of worth. The Gospel confirms this experience; I could never do enough to be worthy. I need something else to give me lasting worth.

- The Gospel offers a worth that is greater than anything I could provide. The Gospel offers me Christ Jesus and says everything that is his can be mine. That far outshines any success I could achieve.

- The Gospel says I can have the greatest worth right now because of Christ. The Gospel doesn't just promise some future reward. No, it says, right now, I am an adopted son of God. God smells on me the fragrance of Christ instead of the stench of my sin. God sees me as having the worth of Christ Jesus himself because I am in Christ. I should rest in that and stop trying to find worth in cheap imposters.

- Because the Gospel is true and at work in my life, I'm set free to work for the Lord. I look to him for my satisfaction, and that means I can go to work for his glory, not my own.

I need to hear the Gospel as much as anyone else. I never stop needing to hear the Gospel applied over and

over again to every part of my life. The better I get at
sharing the Gospel with myself, the better I get at sharing
it with others. In fact, those Gospel truths that I share
with myself are just as true for the unbeliever who is
struggling with the same things I am. The root sins are
the same. I need Jesus as much as the unbeliever does.

What About Preaching Styles?

There are different ways in which pastors pick sermons.
It can be helpful to understand the pros and cons of the
various methods.

Topical

A topical sermon is one where the sermon takes a
particular topic and looks to see what the Bible says about
it. For instance a topical sermon could be titled, "Six
Things the Bible Says about Raising Kids."

Pros: These tend to be highly practical messages for
the congregation.

Cons: It's easier to take verses out of context. Furthermore, difficult or unpopular passages will often be
avoided, so not all Scripture will be preached. It can be
easy to leave the Gospel out of topical sermons.

Expository Preaching

The sermon is based in a particular passage of Scripture. That Scripture drives the main thrust of the sermon.

While the rest of Scripture will be used for interpretation, the sermon examines a particular passage in its context.

Understanding the context of a passage is important because it ensures we use a particular Scripture passage in accordance with God's intent. Philippians 4:13 is often taken out of context. It reads, *"I can do all things through Christ which strengtheneth me"* (King James Version). Some take this verse to mean that they can literally do *all things* through God's strength. Win the football championship? Sure! Close the big sale? Yup! Ask the girl on the date? Certainly!

But when we read the context, we see Paul is speaking of being content in every situation. Paul is not talking about being able to do whatever you want because of Christ's strength. He's speaking of being able to be content in any situation through Christ who gives him strength. A sermon on only Philippians 4:13 could end up leaving the listeners with a misunderstanding of God's intent for this passage.

Topical sermon series can be made up of expository sermons. For instance, the sermons in a topical series on marriage could each be based on a different passage about marriage. The key difference with topical preaching is that in expository preaching a single passage forms the foundation for the sermon.

Pros: This method helps the pastor stay subject to the word instead of using Scripture to just find what he wants. It also allows people to dive deeper into single passages instead of sticking with surface-level overviews.

Cons: It's possible to get so far into the weeds that people miss the big overall flow and storyline of Scripture.

Exegetical Preaching (also called verse-by-verse)

This type of sermon approaches the Bible flatly, almost giving equal weight to every passage. Often pastors will work through just one verse at a time preaching on what is found there. The key difference with this and expository preaching is that exegetical preaching approaches all verses equally, while expository preaching looks to preach units of text and draw out the main themes, not necessarily comment on every single verse.

Pros: This type of sermon goes into great depth. It forces the pastor to look at all topics found in Scripture, not just those that are popular or easy to deal with.

Cons: People can get too lost in the details. It's easier to forget the central thrust of all of Scripture (that it's about Christ).

Children in Worship

One of the most important factors for parents is how their children will fit into the church. Large churches can have children's programs that rival the best daycares. In fact, I know of some parents who go to church mainly so they can have a few hours away from their kids!

But underlying this is often the parents' concern for

their kids. Parents want their kids to go to church because they think it will help them grow into better people. Some parents feel ill equipped to teach their kids. This is a particularly sensitive issue for families that are coming from a different faith. They often see their children's friendships falling away, and they are eager for their kids to make new friends. Before assuming that the best option is to attend a church with bustling kids programs, consider the following items and then make the decision that is best for your family.

God loves your kids more than you.

Putting your kids in an exciting children's program may guarantee they have fun at church while they're young, but it doesn't ensure they will grow up to love God. The only way they can do that is through the Holy Spirit working in their lives. And God loves your kids! Jesus said, *"Let the little children come to me"* (Matt 19:14). We must trust God to care for our children more than any program or lack of program. God works in big churches, and he works in little ones to see children grow up to love him.

When children worship with others, it shows that life is about more than just them.

When children grow up in environments that cater to their needs, they're subtly taught that the world revolves around them. But as we've seen, Christian worship is about taking our eyes off ourselves and putting them upon God. When we don't have our children participate in our worship, we are missing out on one of the few places where people are being taught to look at something bigger than themselves.

It gives your children an opportunity to see how you love God.

Many of us desire to have some type of family devotionals, but it's hard. Life is busy. Participating as a family in worship on Sunday mornings gives our children an opportunity to see your love for God. They notice how we sing and listen to God. They can see and experience our response to the preaching and the sacraments. When they see our eagerness and love of worship, it rubs off on them. If children never worship with us, they miss out on seeing their parents practice what they preach.

There are advantages to churches with huge children's programs, and there are advantages to small churches with little or no kids' programs. I've seen kids grow up loving God in both types of churches, just as I've also seen kids walk away from the faith in both types of churches. A kids' program will not magically ensure your child becomes a Christian.

So don't make a decision about a church solely on the children's programs that are offered.

5
———————

MEMBERSHIP

If you stick around a church for long, you may start to hear talk about membership. Depending upon your background, this could mean different things. And, depending what religious organization you are coming from, the last thing you might want to do is become a member of another church.

Is Membership Biblical?

Critics of church membership like to point out that the Bible never says you must become a member of a church. The idea that the only thing that matters is your relationship with God—that he doesn't care if your name is on a piece of paper—can be very appealing. Some churches abuse membership. Once you become a member, you feel like you can never get away. So what does the Bible say about membership?

Although membership is not explicitly commanded,

we see that it is assumed in some sense within the New Testament. Consider 1 Peter 5:2, *"Be shepherds of God's flock that is under your care, watching over them"* (NIV). Pastors and elders are commanded to shepherd God's flock *that is under [their] care.* This means that a pastor doesn't have a responsibility for every believer, but only those believers who are under his care.

How does he know who is under his care? When does a church visitor come under the care of the pastor? In order for this verse to make sense, some type of membership must be assumed. Otherwise, pastors and elders would not know whom they should shepherd.

In 1 Corinthians 5:12, the Apostle Paul writes, *"It isn't my responsibility to judge outsiders, but it certainly is your responsibility to judge those inside the church who are sinning"* (NLT). This statement implies a knowledge of who is inside versus outside the Church. How do you know who is inside or outside the Church? Membership is probably the most helpful way of clarifying this. One helpful way to think about membership is to think of it as giving a church permission to hold you accountable to Scripture.

Take, for example, a dating couple that visits a church and fills out a visitor information card. The next day the pastor knocks on their door and says, "I noticed that you aren't married, but share the same address. I wanted to come and tell you that you shouldn't be doing that." How do you think this couple would react? Probably not well! Perhaps this couple is not Christian and have no idea of Christian sexual ethics. Perhaps they are brand new

Christians and haven't been taught that Christians should not have sex before marriage. Perhaps they are Christians but have simply drifted away. One thing that is likely is that they will never return to that church or ever fill out another information card.

Now bring Paul's words in 1 Corinthians 5:12 into this scenario. He says that we should not judge outsiders. Why? Because why should we hold others to a Christian standard when they don't accept the same authority that we do? God will certainly judge all people according to his perfect standard. Paul is saying that we shouldn't worry about those outside the Church. God will judge them. We, on the other hand, should want to share the Gospel.

Now, those who are inside the Church should be expected to live according to Christian standards. But is that couple that visited inside or outside the Church? Strictly speaking, they attended church, so they were inside the Church. But I doubt few would interpret it that literally.

What if that couple came four times, or five, or ten? What if they wanted to lead a small group? When do they move from outsiders to insiders? Does the couple become an insider at the same time the church leadership thinks of them as insiders?

This is complicated because we have many in our churches at various places in their own spiritual walk. In my own church, I've had people who considered themselves members from their first Sunday, and others who attended for years before wanting to make a profession of faith and call themselves Christian. Having a clear understanding of membership helps to clarify for everyone who is inside or outside the Church.

What Is Membership?

Membership is simply someone saying, "I believe I'm a Christian," and the local church saying, "Yes, we agree with you." Membership is a protection for both the individual and the church. Again, 1 Corinthians 5:12 is helpful. When someone becomes a member, he or she is saying, "I give permission for this church to speak into my life in matters of following Jesus." When a church accepts someone as a member, it is saying, "We will walk with you on your journey to know Christ."

Formal membership is helpful because everyone is on the same page about expectations. The church doesn't speak into someone's life without first having permission. The individual doesn't expect the church to hold her accountable to the life of a Christian until she publicly professes she is a Christian and becomes a member.

What Is Expected in Membership?

Each church has its own expectation for membership. In our denomination, one does not have to agree with every theological position of our church. We are simply looking for faith in Christ. While we want people to know about our theological beliefs, we only expect those in formal church leadership (pastors, elders, and deacons) to hold to them strictly.

If you become a member in our church, you must answer the following five questions in the affirmative:[1]

1. Do you acknowledge yourselves to be sinners in the sight of God, justly deserving his displeasure, and without hope save [except] in his sovereign mercy?
2. Do you believe in the Lord Jesus Christ as the Son of God, and Savior of sinners, and do you receive and rest upon him alone for salvation as he is offered in the Gospel?
3. Do you now resolve and promise, in humble reliance upon the grace of the Holy Spirit, that you will endeavor to live as becomes the followers of Christ?
4. Do you promise to support the church in its worship and work to the best of your ability?
5. Do you submit yourselves to the government and discipline of the church, and promise to study its purity and peace?

As you see, the bar for membership is not far above what should be expected of any Christian. I would advise caution if a church wants to make the bar for membership much higher than this. Remember our discussion on the unity of the Church? When a church sets a high bar for membership, it also starts to separate itself from God's universal Church.

Now, there may be additional expectations when you become a member. At our church, when we explain the fourth membership vow, we say this means that we expect every member to be worshiping, growing, and giving. This means:

Worshiping

You should make the deliberate worship of God a priority. You should join God's people in worship every Sunday. If you are unable to physically attend a church (because of vacation, sickness, etc.), you should still worship in some way, through listening to a sermon, having family devotions, prayer and singing, etc.

Growing

You should be continually growing in Christ. Our church offers a number of ways to do this through Sunday school, small groups, or other things. Take advantage of these opportunities if you can. If not, make a habit of reading a Christian book or listening to sermons. Each member should be regularly reading the Bible and praying.

Giving

The Church is a community. Each member has been given gifts from God for the blessing of others. So when one person holds back, it hurts the whole church community. God has given us financial resources, so each member should be giving financially. 2 Corinthians 9:6–7 says:

> *Remember this: Whoever sows sparingly will also reap sparingly, and whoever sows generously will also reap generously. Each of you should give what you have decided in your heart to give, not reluctantly or under compulsion, for God loves a cheerful giver.*

We can't tell you what amount is right to give. But if you understand how much God has given you, giving back to him out of joy shows you love and trust God in all things. You should also be giving your time and spiritual gifts. Each member should be serving the church community in some way.

We don't want to have very detailed expectations for membership because Scripture doesn't give detailed expectations. But the question should not be, "What can I skip and still be considered an OK church member?" Rather it should be, "How can I contribute to help this group of people grow together in Christ?" If a church has a long list of membership expectations that seem to go beyond what Scripture says, that may be a cause for concern. Many churches have new member classes. If a church offers that, it is generally a good sign. Attending one of these classes gives you a good idea of what you are signing up for if you become a member. Beware of a church that has no requirements for membership. You might find they have many expectations that they just weren't willing to state publicly.

6

THE MISSION OF THE CHURCH

Why does the Church exist? What would be missing in the world if the Church ceased to exist? Some people wouldn't know what to do with so much free time on Sundays! But seriously, what does the Church contribute to the world? Up to this point, it may seem like we've danced around the answer to this question. However, everything we've looked at supports the Church's mission.

In Matthew 28:18–20, before returning to heaven, Jesus gave his final orders to his disciples:

> *And Jesus came and said to them, "All authority in heaven and on earth has been given to me. Go therefore and make disciples of all nations, baptizing them in the name of the Father and of the Son and of the Holy Spirit, teaching them to observe all that I have commanded you. And behold, I am with you always, to the end of the age." (ESV)*

In the Greek, the main verb and command in this passage is "make disciples." Jesus gave this command to his disciples, but we continue on this mission as those who stand on their foundation (Eph 2:19–20). These disciples died before they could make it to every nation, so the Church continues their work of sharing the Gospel around the globe.

Pastor Mark Dever defines making disciples as "helping others follow Jesus." His definition is helpful because of its simplicity and depth. How Christians practice this depends on who they are discipling. If it is a person who does not know the Gospel, it means helping that person follow Jesus for the first time. If it is a person who has been a Christian his whole life, it means helping that person follow Jesus in some area where he is struggling. In fact, Jesus' two main components of disciple-making were baptism (following him for the first time) and teaching (following him in every area of life).

Unfortunately, the term "discipleship" is one that is often used but rarely understood. Usually there are a few people in a church who are really passionate about making disciples, while most people feel guilty because they feel like they should be but don't know where to start. Some people even feel bad because they *don't* feel bad about their lack of making disciples. The reality is that most people don't get excited when pastors start talking about it. So why should you care to find a church that is passionate about this?

If making disciples were *your* task, it would be overwhelming and discouraging. But Jesus didn't give this task to an individual, he gave it to the Apostles, the foundation of what would become the Church (Eph 2:19–20). This is further evident by primary tasks of the Great Commission: baptism and teaching. Baptism is often performed by ordained ministers. And while everyone has some ability to teach, not everyone is gifted in it or called to do it. But in order for these activities to take place, the Church needs many people who play other vital roles. The person who runs the soundboard and the person who cleans the church after the service contribute to the big goal of making disciples.

My friend Brian Tsui, who ministers among many first-and-second generation immigrants at San Jose State University, says simply showing up to church helps to fulfill the Great Commission. To the students he brings to church (many of whom have never set foot in a Christian church), just seeing believers there speaks volumes to them. It shows that people believe that what is happening at a church service is important enough to give up a good chunk of their Sunday morning. This doesn't minimize the need for everyone to be able to explain the Gospel and why they believe it (1 Pet 3:25), but it does mean the burden for accomplishing the Great Commission does not fall on the individual's shoulders.

We can think of the great commission in light of 1 Corinthians 12, where Paul likens the Church to a body with various parts and functions that all support the whole. In other words, no one person can fulfill the Great Commission by herself. It takes a church (the body of Christ) to make a disciple.

If making disciples is the core mission of the Church, how does this fit into God's bigger story of what he is doing in the world? In his book *The Kingdom of God and the Church,* Geerhardus Vos wrote, "The Church actually has within herself the powers of the world to come.... She forms an intermediate link between the present life and the life of eternity."[1] This is exciting! The powers of the world to come! An intermediate link between the present life and the life of eternity! This sounds like the stuff of science fiction, but it's not—God *plans* to unite all things in Christ.

For all those I have lost, let me rephrase: the heaven we long for has broken into this present age, and it has happened through the Church. This means those who are part of the Church have front row seats to God's grand work to unite all things in Christ!

One of God's promises in the Old Testament was that this current world, broken by sin, would be replaced by the New Creation. God would do a second work of creation (or recreation), making a world that is better than the first. It would be better because there will be no mark of sin—or even the possibility of sin—entering again (Isa 34:4, 51:6, 56:5, 65:17).

When Jesus begins his ministry in Luke 4 he reads from the scroll of Isaiah a passage (Isa 61) that describes the New Creation, ushered in by the Messiah. In this new world, the poor are encouraged, the blind see, the captives are set free. There are no more tears or pain there (Rev 21:4). Jesus then tells his listeners something unbelievable: this promise of the New Creation was fulfilled when Jesus read those words from Isaiah!

How do we make sense of Jesus' words regarding the fulfillment of the promised New Creation? It makes sense when we consider them in light of his whole life. Jesus, though fully God, was also fully human. His life mirrored ours in every way, even in dying. In one sense Jesus' life was very ordinary. But three days after his death something remarkable happened. He was raised from the dead! If we are thinking of the Church as the future, we cannot miss the significance of this.

Paul explains it in 1 Corinthians 15. He states that Jesus' resurrection was the first taste of the resurrection (1 Cor 15:20); when he returns, all those who belong to Christ will be raised from the dead. This means that the end-times resurrection started with Christ. If Christ still lay in the grave, we would still be waiting for God to begin making all things new. But we aren't still waiting. Three days later God resurrected Christ. And that was the turning point. A new work was afoot, a work of recreation, the work of making all things new. It was the beginning of the end. The resurrection of Christ was the spark that started the fire that will one day fill all the world with its light!

Christ is living the resurrection life that we also will live. To put it another way, Christ, in his resurrection body, is the first person to experience New Creation. This New Creation, that place described in Revelation 21 and 22, is not something fully in the future. The heavenly New Creation broke into our Old Creation when Jesus Christ was raised from the dead.

Now, here is where it gets even more exciting. Paul tells us in 2 Corinthians 5:17, *"Therefore, if anyone is in Christ, he is a new creation. The old has passed away; behold, the new has come."* Paul teaches that those who have faith in Christ are united to Christ. A function of that union with Christ is that, just as Christ was made new in the resurrection, so also are Christians made new in Christ's image. Paul teaches us that when you become a Christian, you are spiritually resurrected. You take on a New Creation spirit, a spirit that is part of the new heavens and new earth.

Think of it as a spark. The New Creation spirit in your life may be just a spark, but Jesus will not *"crush the weakest reed or put out a flickering candle"* (Isa 42:3). The source of this flicker is a fire that originates not in this world, but has come (time traveled!?) from the future New Creation into your present life. The future has broken into the present!

So the mission of the Church, making disciples, has cosmic implications. It's the conduit through which people experience the joy of New Creation. Before a military operation, one unit—usually the one with the strongest commander—is designated as the "main effort." This unit is responsible for the most crucial part of the mission, and the surrounding units support them.

The Church (God's people) is the "unit" God has designated as the main effort. Christ has bought the Church with his blood, and God has equipped the

Church with his Spirit. We have been given spiritual gifts in order to accomplish our mission of making disciples. The Church is where the action is. Your service to God, no matter how big or small, is of infinite value, because you are helping to build something that will last forever.

The Church is uniquely equipped and commissioned for this task; no one else can do this. If the Church is distracted with other things, no one else will pick up the slack. This mission may not seem exciting, but the transformation that occurs when someone follows Jesus is one of the most amazing things in the world. Paralyzing fear is transformed into trust. Regret and anger are transformed into peace. Lost innocence is transformed into hope in God's promise to make all things new. The Church is tasked with the work of transforming the dead into the living, and nothing is more exciting than that!

AFTERWORD

Congratulations! You've made it to the end. By now you should have found just the right church for you! Right? Perhaps the search has been easy. Perhaps it has left more questions. There is beauty in the diversity of churches, but that can also be frustrating. Let me leave you with a few closing thoughts as you seek to find a church.

No Church Is Perfect

It's unlikely you will find a church that will perfectly fit every one of your desires. Every church has flaws. The longer you stay at a church the more you may see its flaws. But every church has its strengths as well. You can think of it like a marriage. Your spouse has flaws, but there are also those things that attracted you to him or her. Does the good outweigh the bad? If you are looking for a perfect church, you will be looking your whole life.

God can still work in big ways through flawed

churches. God has a history of working through fallen people and institutions. A particular church's imperfections won't stop God from accomplishing his purposes. In fact, it is through the very weaknesses of the church that God's power is displayed. When people see this they wonder how could such good come from such flawed and weak people!

God works through ordinary means to bring about extraordinary change. This is good news because we are ordinary people! Our spiritual growth isn't tied to how rocking the music is, how many Bible studies the church has, or how dynamic the preaching is. None of these things are bad. They can be great blessings. But they are only the icing on the cake. God works through his Word and Spirit, and God's Word and Spirit work through very ordinary things!

Ephesians 4 is helpful if you are struggling to find a church. Verse 13 outlines God's goal for his Church: *"We all reach unity in the faith and in the knowledge of the Son of God and become mature, attaining to the whole measure of the fullness of Christ."* God's goal is for *all* his people to obtain the *"whole measure of the fullness of Christ."* This means God isn't excited by someone who speeds off alone on a spiritual journey because he doesn't want to be held up by others. God's goal requires community. It's a team effort. He cares about the spiritual growth of every one of his people.

If you never plug into a church because of its flaws, how does that help all his people reach the fullness of Christ? Perhaps he is calling you to help in a church particularly because of its weaknesses. Indeed, doesn't this relate to the basic message of the Gospel itself? Christ committed himself to us not because we were perfect, but because we were deeply flawed. And he did that in order to make us beautiful in his sight. We were loved while we were sinners. Now we must love others who are sinful.

If you are struggling to find the right church, I'd encourage you to remember Ephesians 2:22. It reads, *"And in him you too are being built together to become a dwelling in which God lives by his Spirit."* This passage describes how God is building his home. In the Old Testament, God's home on earth was his temple. Only the finest materials were used: gold, silver, cedar, and olive wood. But this was a temporary home, a summer place to spend a few weeks of the year. The home in Ephesians 2:22, however, is God's eternal home.

And how much more do those materials matter? And what is God using? Us—you and me! People, broken, flawed, and sinful, yet made beautiful by the life-giving spirit of Christ. So remember, the people you struggle to get along with at church? God thinks they are worthy of use in his eternal home. If God loves others like this, how can we not?

The Church Is a Family

When you follow Christ you gain a new family. Jesus points out in Matthew 12 that those who do his Father's will are his family. While we do get to choose a church, we don't get to choose who is in that church, just like you don't get to choose your family. There will always be a few crazy aunts in every family... and in every church! But the key to a healthy family is love. It's the same with the church.

In Mark 10:29–31 Jesus says:

> *Truly I tell you no one who has left home or brothers or sisters or mother or father or children or fields for me and the gospel will fail to receive a hundred times as much in this present age: homes, brothers, sisters, mothers, children and fields—along with persecutions —and in the age to come eternal life.*

Jesus gives a promise in this life, that when we follow Christ we get a new family. For some, following Christ will have a high cost. Others will never have experienced family in a healthy way. Some will find that their families join them on this faith journey. But no matter one's circumstances, Jesus promises you will gain a new and better family when you follow him.

Jesus doesn't minimize our biological families. He expands the idea of family to make it so much more. God deeply cares about family, so much so that he wants everyone to be able to experience it. God places the lonely in families (Ps 68:6). This means that if we chose a church because we want something good just for our biological families, we are missing the whole point. Instead, being part of the Church plugs your family into a much larger one—the family of God. A local church may be the first loving family some people experience. Those with good families should recognize that these are only teasers of the better family that awaits us in God, and we should open up so more can experience that blessing.

In a healthy church, anyone should be able to find people who love them, help carry their burdens, and care for them as a family should. In a good church, outsiders are invited into homes for family dinners. Not necessarily perfect, Instagram-worthy dinners, but family dinners, where the food is a backdrop to the people that gather around the table. In summary, the Church is a family because God has unified us by the blood of Jesus. It's important to find a church where you will be welcomed like family, and it's equally important that you open up your life to care for others in the church community.

You Won't Feel at Home Unless You Get Involved

It's hard to get to know people by just spending an hour or two with them on a Sunday morning. If you never take the next step and go to Sunday school classes or small groups or other events, you will never really feel at home. If you develop friendships at your church, you are much more likely to be happy.

Don't Sacrifice More Important Things for Lesser Things

Back when I was single, I'd just moved to a new town and was eager to find a church with young people my age. In particular, I was looking for a church with pretty, single women! After visiting a few, I found one that had a group of people in their twenties. Although I didn't really connect with the pastor or feel welcomed by many in the church, it had the one thing I was really looking for at that time, so it matched my criteria. I thought I was set, and I was ready for a ton of dates.

After about eight months at the church, I found myself getting more and more frustrated and wanting less and less to attend that church. I ended up going back to another church I'd initially rejected because there was no one my age. But the preaching was better, and I felt more welcome. I ended up growing much more in Christ in this church. It was also during this time that I met my wife. I learned to keep the important things important while seeking a church, and that God will take care of the details.

You Don't Have to Stay in One Church Forever

While many Americans have far too low a commitment to a church, it's also good to remember that you don't have to stay in one church forever. If you've followed this guide in finding a church, you've likely found a church that fits within the sphere of the true Church. These churches are all part of God's one Church. And while leaving a church should never be a light matter, there can be good reasons to leave one church for another. Your own theological convictions may change, or you move to a different part of town, or you feel called to help a new church start, for example. Before leaving, you should talk with other Christians to get their advice. If you are leaving for good reasons, that church should celebrate how God is working in your life. It's helpful to keep this in mind, especially when you are leaving one that believes it is the only true Church.

The Church Is a Community

When you finally join a church, celebrate! You are joining a community of people who are broken, loving and trying to walk through this life in a way that honors Christ. Many of your best friends will be made in a church. Your children will develop great friendships and have unforgettable memories.

The Church is beautiful and messy, but it is also built upon the foundations of Christ. The Church is most healthy when its people are most submitting themselves to Christ's lordship. You have the ability to make your new church a better place. You have the ability to use your gifts to help others. Let me leave you with a final picture of the Church. Keep this picture in mind, because sometimes the Church seems far from this ideal, but don't give up. God is faithful, and he will finish what he has started.

This will continue until we all come to such unity in our faith and knowledge of God's Son that we will be mature in the Lord, measuring up to the full and complete standard of Christ. (Eph 4:13, NLT)

APPENDIX 1

CHURCH VISITATION SURVEY

Essentials

1. Does the church uphold the basics (the DIE category) of the faith? These basics of the faith are outlined in the historic creeds (Apostles' Creed, Nicene Creed, etc.).
2. Is the church focused on making disciples?
3. Did the worship point us to God and his glory?
4. Was the sermon centered on the Gospel?
5. Does the church see Scripture (Old and New Testament) as its final authority?
6. Will the church care for me (and my family) on our spiritual walk?
7. Does the church keep the important things important or get sidetracked by side issues?

Nice-to-Haves

1. Was I welcomed?
2. Are there people in my age group?
3. Does the church reflect the community it is in?
4. Is there an appropriate level of diversity for where the church is located? (Age, education level, ethnicity, etc.)
5. Is the church close?
6. Are there people in the church who live close to me?

Icing on the Cake

1. Do I agree with the church on less important theological matters?
2. Do I like the worship style?
3. Are there programs for me and my kids?
4. Does the church have good facilities?

APPENDIX 2

HISTORIC CREEDS AND CONFESSIONS

The Apostles' Creed [300s AD]

This creed gets its name not because it was written by the apostles, but because it dates back to the earliest times of the church. The term "catholic" with a lowercase "c" refers not to a particular denomination, but to the universal church.

I believe in God, the Father Almighty,
the Maker of heaven and earth,
and in Jesus Christ, His only Son, our Lord:
Who was conceived by the Holy Ghost,
born of the virgin Mary,
suffered under Pontius Pilate,
was crucified, dead, and buried;
He descended into hell.
The third day He arose again from the dead;

He ascended into heaven,
and sitteth on the right hand of God the Father
Almighty;
from thence he shall come to judge the quick and
the dead.
I believe in the Holy Ghost;
the holy catholic church;
the communion of saints;
the forgiveness of sins;
the resurrection of the body;
and the life everlasting.
Amen.

The Nicene Creed [325 AD]

I believe in one God, the Father Almighty, Maker of
heaven and earth, and of all things visible and invisible.
And in one Lord Jesus Christ, the only-begotten Son of
God, begotten of the Father before all worlds; God of
God, Light of Light, very God of very God; begotten, not
made, being of one substance with the Father, by whom
all things were made.
Who, for us men and for our salvation, came down from
heaven, and was incarnate by the Holy Spirit of the
virgin Mary, and was made man; and was crucified also
for us under Pontius Pilate; He suffered and was buried;
and the third day He rose again, according to the Scriptures; and ascended into heaven, and sits on the right
hand of the Father; and He shall come again, with glory,

to judge the quick and the dead; whose kingdom shall have no end.

And I believe in the Holy Ghost, the Lord and Giver of Life; who proceeds from the Father and the Son; who with the Father and the Son together is worshiped and glorified; who spoke by the prophets.

And I believe in one holy catholic and apostolic Church. I acknowledge one baptism for the remission of sins; and I look for the resurrection of the dead, and the life of the world to come. Amen.

The Athanasian Creed [500s AD]

Whosoever will be saved, before all things it is necessary that he hold the catholic faith. Which faith except everyone do keep whole and undefiled, without doubt he shall perish everlastingly. And the catholic faith is this: That we worship one God in Trinity, and Trinity in Unity, neither confounding the persons, nor dividing the substance.

For there is one Person of the Father, another of the Son, and another of the Holy Spirit. But the godhead of the Father, of the Son, and of the Holy Spirit, is all one, the glory equal, the majesty co-eternal.

Such as the Father is, such is the Son, and such is the Holy Spirit. The Father uncreated, the Son uncreated, and the Holy Spirit uncreated. The Father incomprehensible, the Son incomprehensible, and the Holy Spirit incomprehensible.

The Father eternal, the Son eternal, and the Holy Spirit eternal. And yet they are not three eternals, but one Eternal.

As also there are not three incomprehensibles, nor three uncreated, but one Uncreated, and one Incomprehensible. So likewise the Father is Almighty, the Son Almighty, and the Holy Spirit Almighty. And yet they are not three almighties, but one Almighty.

So the Father is God, the Son is God, and the Holy Spirit is God. And yet they are not three gods, but one God.

So likewise the Father is Lord, the Son Lord, and the Holy Spirit Lord. And yet not three lords, but one Lord. For as we are compelled by the Christian verity to acknowledge each Person by Himself to be both God and Lord, so we are also forbidden by the catholic religion to say that there are three gods or three lords.

The Father is made of none, neither created, nor begotten. The Son is of the Father alone, not made, nor created, but begotten. The Holy Spirit is of the Father, neither made, nor created, nor begotten, but proceeding. So there is one Father, not three fathers; one Son, not three sons; one Holy Spirit, not three holy spirits.

And in the Trinity none is before or after another; none is greater or less than another, but all three Persons are co-eternal together and co-equal. So that in all things, as is aforesaid, the Unity in Trinity and the Trinity in Unity is to be worshiped.

He therefore that will be saved must think thus of the Trinity.

Furthermore, it is necessary to everlasting salvation that

he also believe rightly the Incarnation of our Lord Jesus Christ. For the right faith is, that we believe and confess, that our Lord Jesus Christ, the Son of God, is God and man; God, of the substance of the Father, begotten before the worlds; and man of the substance of his mother, born in the world; perfect God and perfect man, of a rational soul and human flesh subsisting. Equal to the Father, as touching His godhead; and inferior to the Father, as touching His manhood; who, although He is God and man, yet he is not two, but one Christ; one, not by conversion of the godhead into flesh but by taking of the manhood into God; one altogether; not by confusion of substance, but by unity of person. For as the rational soul and flesh is one man, so God and man is one Christ; who suffered for our salvation, descended into hell, rose again the third day from the dead. He ascended into heaven, He sits at the right hand of the Father, God Almighty, from whence He will come to judge the quick and the dead. At His coming all men will rise again with their bodies and shall give account for their own works. And they that have done good shall go into life everlasting; and they that have done evil into everlasting fire.

This is the catholic faith, which except a man believe faithfully, he cannot be saved.

The Chicago Statement of Biblical Inerrancy [1978]

While not a historic creed, this statement is widely

regarded as one of the best summaries of the doctrine of inerrancy.

1. God, who is Himself Truth and speaks truth only, has inspired Holy Scripture in order thereby to reveal Himself to lost mankind through Jesus Christ as Creator and Lord, Redeemer and Judge. Holy Scripture is God's witness to Himself.

2. Holy Scripture, being God's own Word, written by men prepared and superintended by His Spirit, is of infallible divine authority in all matters upon which it touches: it is to be believed, as God's instruction, in all that it affirms: obeyed, as God's command, in all that it requires; embraced, as God's pledge, in all that it promises.

3. The Holy Spirit, Scripture's divine Author, both authenticates it to us by His inward witness and opens our minds to understand its meaning.

4. Being wholly and verbally God-given, Scripture is without error or fault in all its teaching, no less in what it states about God's acts in creation, about the events of world history, and about its own literary origins under God, than in its witness to God's saving grace in individual lives.

5. The authority of Scripture is inescapably impaired if this total divine inerrancy is in any way limited or disregarded, or made relative to a view of truth contrary to the Bible's own; and such lapses bring serious loss to both the individual and the Church.

ENDNOTES

Chapter 2: What Makes a True Church?

1. I reference different translations of the Bible in this booklet. Unless noted otherwise, the New International Version is used. I use other translations for the sake of clarity or familiarity. But certainly you are free to use whatever translation is most familiar to you in your own study.
2. There are two times when a church may ask for someone to be re-baptized. First, some churches will not accept the baptism of someone who was baptized as an infant, even if it was in a church that subscribes to the same essential doctrines. Second, some churches will only accept baptisms that are done by immersion. In my opinion, these restrictions go beyond what Scripture says regarding baptism and hurt the unity of the church that we seek to proclaim.
3. I realize the term Trinity can be a stumbling block,

especially for those coming from an LDS background. For the sake of this book, I'd encourage you to keep reading to see how the Trinity plays a crucial role in this discussion about churches. A good introduction to the Trinity is R.C. Sproul's booklet *What Is the Trinity?*.

4. "Unsatisfied Persecuted Church Member to Try Out Other Church Just across Minefield," Babylonbee.com, June 8, 2016, http://babylonbee.com/news/unsatisfied-persecuted-church-member-try-church-just-across-minefield/.

Chapter 3: Diversity in Churches

1. For more information on the canon see *The Heresy of Orthodoxy: How Contemporary Culture's Fascination with Diversity Has Reshaped Our Understanding of Early Christianity*

2. The verb *was* in English is past tense, but the Greek word used here is imperfect, which means something true in the past that continues to the present.

Chapter 4: Worship Explained

1. This breakdown of the elements of worship comes from *Gather God's People: Understand, Plan, and Lead Worship in Your Local Church* by Brian Croft and Jason Adkins.

Chapter 5: Membership

1. The Book of Church Order of the Presbyterian Church in America, 57-5

Chapter 6: The Mission of the Church

1. Geerhardus Vos, *The Teaching of Jesus Concerning the Kingdom of God and the Church*. Nutley, NJ: Presbyterian and Reformed, 1972, p. 84.

25339653R00065

Made in the USA
Columbia, SC
30 August 2018